HOORAY FOR TEACHERS!

by Elle Parkes

BUMBA BOOKS™

LERNER PUBLICATIONS ◆ MINNEAPOLIS

Note to Educators:

Throughout this book, you'll find critical thinking questions. These can be used to engage young readers in thinking critically about the topic and in using the text and photos to do so.

Lerner Publications Company
A division of Lerner Publishing Group, Inc.
241 First Avenue North
Minneapolis, MN 55401 USA

For reading levels and more information, look up this title at www.lernerbooks.com.

Library of Congress Cataloging-in-Publication Data

Names: Parkes, Elle, author.
Title: Hooray for teachers! / by Elle Parkes.
Description: Minneapolis, MN : Lerner Publications, 2016. | Series: Bumba books—Hooray for community helpers! | Includes bibliographical references and index.
Identifiers: LCCN 2015043698 (print) | LCCN 2016004350 (ebook) | ISBN 9781512414370 (lb : alk. paper) | ISBN 9781512414653 (pb : alk. paper) ISBN 9781512414660 (eb pdf)
Subjects: LCSH: Teachers—Juvenile literature.
Classification: LCC LB1775 .P37 2016 (print) | LCC LB1775 (ebook) | DDC 371.102—dc23

LC record available at http://lccn.loc.gov/2015043698

Manufactured in the United States of America
1 – VP – 7/15/16

Expand learning beyond the printed book. Download free, complementary educational resources for this book from our website, www.lerneresource.com.

Table of Contents

Teachers Help Students

Teachers work at schools.

They teach students

new things.

A teacher works in a classroom.

This room has desks and chairs.

How do you think it helps students to have their own desks?

Gym teachers work in

a gym.

They teach students

sports and games.

This teacher teaches how

to play basketball.

Teachers know many subjects.

They help students learn.

They give students tests.

Some teachers teach different subjects.

This teacher only teaches art.

She shows how to cut shapes.

Why do you think some teachers only teach one subject?

13

Teachers teach in fun ways.

They use movies and music.

This teacher uses computers

to teach music.

What do you think are other fun ways teachers teach?

Teachers work long days.

They watch students during recess.

They meet with parents

after school.

Teachers go to college.

They study hard.

They learn for four years or more.

Teachers work with many students.

Students learn in different ways.

Teachers help all students learn.

Teacher Tools

whiteboard

markers

pencils

desk

books

computer

tablet

Picture Glossary

classroom

a room in a school where classes take place

college

a place to continue studying after high school

recess

a break from school

students

people who study at a school

23

Index

Read More

De Nijs, Erika. *A Teacher's Job.* New York: Cavendish Square Publishing, 2016.

Heos, Bridget. *Let's Meet a Teacher.* Minneapolis: Millbrook Press, 2013.

Siemens, Jared. *Teachers.* New York: AV2 by Weigl, 2016.

Photo Credits